365 Daily Do Its
Organizing Tips and Challenges to Help You Get (and Stay) Organized Throughout the Year

First Edition - COPYRIGHT 2016 by Christina Scalise
All rights reserved. No part of this publication may be reproduced, distributed or transmitted in any form or by any means, including photocopying, recording, or any other electronic or mechanical methods, without the prior written permission of the publisher and copyright owner.

Published by... Christina Scalise, Author of Organize Your Life and More and owner and creator of... OrganizeYourLifeAndMore.com, 405 Spain Gulf Rd. North, Poland, NY 13431

Cover Design by Canva.com

CONTENTS

Introduction

Daily Do Its for the month of...

- ✓ January
- ✓ February
- ✓ March
- ✓ April
- ✓ May
- ✓ June
- ✓ July
- ✓ August
- ✓ September
- ✓ October
- ✓ November
- ✓ December

About the Author

Introduction

So... what are Daily Do It's you ask? Daily Do Its are daily organizing tips and challenges that help you get organized throughout the year in a way that will ALSO help you maintain organization for years to come. Some are quick and easy; and some are more challenging than others. You may notice a few Daily Do Its have been repeated more than once throughout the year. The reason for this is simple...those particular tasks should become a habitual part of your organizing routine.

How it works: Do each daily task (every month) as shown - OR - each month, simply choose the tasks that are most important to you and get those done. For the ones that do not apply to you... use those days to choose a different Daily Do It that does apply to you - OR - do one or more things on your personal To Do list - OR - simply take an extra day off for yourself and enjoy what you've already organized.

It's completely up to YOU!
- If you want to challenge yourself...do as many as you can.
- If you want to be more organized in certain areas of your life and/or home...choose the ones that you think will be the most beneficial.
- If you just want to improve your organizational skills, and maybe learn a few great organizing tips along the way...read through and mark those that interest you.

And, if you miss a day, it's okay; just start again tomorrow. Remember, you don't HAVE to do every one as shown. It's like going to the gym...yes, it's better to keep up with it each day if you'd like the most beneficial results. But, YOU are in control and can choose how much you'd like to get done. And, you can always start over again and do a little more to catch up (if you want to).

Bottom line... YOU CAN <u>*DO IT!!!*</u> YOU CAN get organized!

Before you start: Add a few minutes (or more) to your daily schedule so you'll be sure to have enough time to accomplish each task. The most common excuse for NOT getting organized is... *"I don't have time!"* But, the fact remains, the more organized you are, the more time you will save.

Remember... *"Organization isn't about perfection; it's about efficiency, reducing stress and clutter, saving time and money and improving your overall quality of life. " – Christina Scalise, Organize Your Life and More....* so let's have fun with it!

*** Please note: 365 Daily Do Its is a wonderful addition to the book...Organize Your Life and More by Christina Scalise, but you do <u>not</u> have to have that book, to complete each daily task.

Wishing you the best in organizing success!
- Christina Scalise

Ready? Set? GO!!! Happy New Year! January is National Get Organized Month... so let's start out THIS year right...by getting (and staying) organized! Let's set aside some time in our busy schedules (each day or week) for reducing clutter, organizing and figure out which areas of our lives (or homes) need the most organizing. Walk around your home and find where clutter is accumulating the most and which areas are lacking storage; and also think about your schedules and finances. Then, check the Daily Do Its list each day and start prioritizing. Choose one or more tasks and mark them off as you go... the quicker you accomplish each task, the more time you will have at the end of each month to sit back and enjoy what you've already organized.

January is...
National Get Organized month / Clean Out Your Closets month / Financial Wellness month
Second Monday in January is...
National Clean off Your Desk Day
Last full week of January...
National Clean Out Your Inbox week

1/1: Place a "Discard Basket" or "Toss Bucket" in a common area of your home (such as a hallway or laundry room) for all family members to contribute unwanted items to daily... or, give each family member a basket of their own to fill. Every time a basket is filled, take time to empty it. Then toss, donate or sell those items as soon as possible.

1/2: Look through the closets in your home. Find new ways to reorganize and utilize lost storage space; stack items vertically, add or move a shelf, regroup like items together, place smaller items in containers, hang things up and get rid of those items you no longer want or need.

✓ **1/3:** Create a family budget; list all finances including income, monthly expenses, loan balances, interest rates, financial goals and more. * *Check out Chapter 12 ("Finances") of Organize Your Life and More for more information on how to create a family budget... examples are shown.*

✓ **1/4:** Create (or update) a cleaning schedule and (if necessary) add each task to your daily/weekly/monthly events calendar as a reminder.

✓ **1/5:** Take down all holiday decorations and store them away. Get rid of any you no longer want or need.

✓ **1/6:** Gather all paperwork needed to file your taxes and set them aside in one clearly labeled box or file until you are ready to use them. If you have not already done so, create a new file for next year's taxes and add all necessary paperwork to it throughout the year.

✓ **1/7:** Too many accounts to keep track of? Simplify your finances by finding accounts that are no longer beneficial to you and close them out. Ask your accountant or financial advisor for help, if necessary.

✓ **1/8:** Do you have any clothes in need of repair? Missing buttons? Maybe a small hole that needs to be fixed on your favorite shirt? Repair any clothing items that need it today...or bring them to someone who can.

✓ **1/9:** Clean off your desk as much as possible today and then organize the remaining items.

✓ **1/10:** Organize all dresser drawers today. Toss, sell or donate any unwanted items.

✓ **1/11:** Clean your closet today; remove all unwanted and unused items, wipe down shelves, vacuum and dust the entire area.

✓ **1/12:** Go through your closet and get rid of any items that are unwanted, outdated, worn out or no longer fit...pants, shoes, shirts, coats, hats, scarves, gloves and more.

✓ **1/13:** Sharpen all pencils and test all pens and markers both in your home and at work. Toss those that are no longer usable.

✓ **1/14:** Organize one drawer in your home office area today.

✓ **1/15:** Search your home and try to find five or more items (clothes, knick-knacks, gadgets, coffee mugs, books, movies, etc.) your family no longer wants or needs; then toss, sell or donate those items.

✓ **1/16:** Purchase, recycle or repurpose one item today that will help you organize the things on top of your desk.

✓ **1/17:** Go through each piece of incoming mail every day...shred, toss, file or respond if necessary. If it's not possible to deal with certain ones right away, schedule in a day/time to take care of them soon.

✓ **1/18:** Keep track of EVERY expense you have this week...groceries, gas, supplies, restaurant meals, entertainment, etc. Do this for an entire month (or more) and then total up each expense category when you are done. The results may surprise you.

✓ **1/19:** Repair, replace or toss one broken item in your home today.

✔ **1/20:** Choose one or more cabinets to clean out today (kitchen, laundry room, bathroom, etc.) Take everything out, wipe down each shelf, get rid of unwanted items, group like items together and then place everything back into the cabinet in an organized manner.

✔ **1/21:** Create a morning checklist for everyone in the family...what needs to be done and what NOT to forget. Example: feed the dog, take out the garbage don't forget your cellphone, homework and lunch.

✔ **1/22:** Find one or more items in your home that have been sitting out for awhile and put them away where they belong...for items that don't have a designated storage spot, create one.

✔ **1/23:** Clean out your basement today. Toss all unwanted items, dust and wipe down shelves and organize the remaining items. If you don't have a basement, clean out another large area of your home in need of organization.

✔ **1/24:** What area of your life could benefit the most from being organized...your home, office, time management, schedule, finances? Work on improving those areas today.

✔ **1/25:** Clear the papers off of your desk at work and at home today. Shred, file, toss or do the necessary task associated with each piece of paper. If you can't deal with something right away, schedule in time to take care of it this week or as soon as possible.

✔ **1/26:** Go through your email inbox and unsubscribe to those you no longer want to receive. Then, respond to, delete or file as many emails as possible.

✎ **1/27:** Find more time... create a schedule that will work well for everyone, share household chores, combine shopping trips and learn how to say "no thank you" more often to events and get togethers you really don't care to attend. *For more time saving tips – check out Chapter 10 of Organize Your Life and More.*

✎ **1/28:** Take the day off today, enjoy what you've already organized and spend some time with friends and/or family.

✎ **1/29:** Share with a friend or family member, your best organizing tip and then ask for theirs in exchange.

✎ **1/30:** Offer to help someone do an organizing / cleaning project in exchange for their help with one of your projects.

✎ **1/31:** Do one or more things on your personal To Do list today.

February is...
Archive Your Files month
Second Monday in February is...
Clean Out Your Computer Day

✍ **2/1:** Start planning / shopping for Valentine's Day.

✍ **2/2:** Add some time to your schedule for family and loved ones today. Plan romantic getaways with your significant other (even if it's something as simple as a night out to dinner and the movies) and schedule in some fun activities each week for the kids.

✍ **2/3:** Set up a mail station with all mailing supplies placed together in one central location...stamps, envelopes, return address labels, etc.

✍ **2/4:** Set up a bill paying station next to your mail station with everything you need for paying bills....unpaid bills, pending receipts, a copy of your budget, calculator, etc.

✍ **2/5:** Dust all picture frames, knick-knacks, hanging lights and baseboards.

✍ **2/6:** Organize and prioritize your cell phone apps and computer shortcuts into easy to find categories.

✍ **2/7:** Find a stack of papers that have been sitting around for a while and take care of each piece of paper in that pile immediately...recycle, toss, shred, file or finish any necessary tasks related to the papers involved.

✍ **2/8:** Delete all programs and computer files you no longer need. Then, organize the remaining files into appropriately labeled digital folders.

✔ **2/9:** Go vertical...create more storage space by stacking a few things vertically instead of horizontally today.

✔ **2/10:** Search your home and try to find five or more items (clothes, knick-knacks, gadgets, coffee mugs, books, movies, etc.) your family no longer wants or needs; then toss, sell or donate those items.

✔ **2/11:** Dispose of any older personal care items that have expired or you no longer use such as...cosmetics, deodorant, toothpaste, shaving supplies, nail and hair care products. *Note: small baskets and containers are a great way to store the smaller products you want to keep.*

✔ **2/12:** Choose one room in your home and clean the entire room from top to bottom. Clean the baseboards, windows, walls, floors, furniture and light fixtures, get rid of any unwanted items and for each item you find that does not have a storage place; create one.

✔ **2/13:** Set up a filing system for your receipts today...or update an existing one.

✔ **2/14:** Take the day off today, enjoy what you've already organized and spend some time with friends and/or family.

✔ **2/15:** Update the information in your address book, rolodex, cell phone and/or email accounts. Delete the contacts you no longer need.

✔ **2/16:** Find one or more items in your home that have been sitting out for awhile and put them away where they belong...for items that don't have a designated storage spot, create one.

2/17: Do you have a box or file labeled "Miscellaneous"? If so, go through the items inside and find a more appropriate place to store each item - OR – simply label the box or file with a detailed description of <u>every</u> item inside.

2/18: Go through the files in your file cabinet and toss or shred the ones that are outdated and no longer needed. Then, position your remaining files in a way that you can easily read each tab and make sure they are placed in the correct order (alphabetical, by subject matter, etc.). *For more information on "Questions to Ask Yourself Before Throwing Away Papers" and "What and When to Toss" please refer to Chapter 13 ("Paperwork") of Organize Your Life and More.*

2/19: Do one or more things on your personal To Do list today.

2/20: Create a Manuals/Product Information file folder. And, if necessary, separate that file into subfolder categories such as; large appliances, outdoor equipment, household products, personal items and toys. If you already have a Manuals/Product Information file, go through it and toss the ones you no longer need.

2/21: Walk around your home and find a few things that need to be labeled...boxes, drawers, file cabinets, storage containers and more. Don't forget to check the garage, attic and cellar areas as well. *Note:* **Remember.... SEE IT = FIND IT** *...if you cannot see each item without digging inside a box, drawer, file cabinet or storage container, adding clearly written labels (describing the contents inside) will help save a lot of wasted time searching for lost items.*

2/22: Sort through your greeting cards, toss the ones you no longer want to keep and organize the rest into a small filing system (Birthday, Anniversary, Get Well, Holiday, etc.).

2/23: Clean/dust all of the fans in your home today.

2/24: Find an unused decorative container or basket that has been sitting around for awhile and find a good use for it...organize small items, decorate your home (fill it with potpourri, pinecones or dried flowers) or store your pet's favorite toys in it (be sure to place it in an area where your pet(s) can reach it).

2/25: Create a clearly written How To instruction sheet for an item in your home that you and/or your family members need help with often, then post it in an area close to that item. Example: A child needs instructions on how to use the washing machine...write them down and hang them near the washing machine where they can be refered to often.

2/26: Have each family member find one or more items they no longer want or need and toss, sell or donate those items immediately.

2/27: Go through your digital pictures today (computer, cell phone, digital frame). Are there any you would like to delete? Can you organize them into folders ...by person, category or subject matter?

2/28: Go through the supplies in your laundry room. Get rid of the items you no longer need then organize the remaining items together into categories such as... detergent, fabric softeners, stain fighters, etc.

2/29 (Leap Year bonus)**:** Consider going digital with your documents. Recipes, receipts and more can all be scanned and saved into a computer. Don't forget to back up your files when you're done.

March is...

Supply Management month / Optimism month
First two weeks of March (specific dates are set each year)...
National Procrastination week
Second Tuesday of March is...
Organize Your Home Office Day
Last week of March is... National Cleaning week

3/1: In honor of Optimism month, make it a point to start thinking more positively. Incorporate a sense of humor into everything you do, avoid negative self-talk and tackle one small job at a time. You CAN do it! You CAN get organized!

3/2: Consider hiding a small amount of cash somewhere in your car for unplanned expenses. A simple $20 bill tucked away in the glove compartment may come in handy one day.

3/3: Clean out your junk drawer. Toss what you no longer need and find alternate storage places for items that do not belong; then organize the remaining items. *For more detailed instructions on "How to Organize a Junk Drawer", please see Chapter 8 of Organize Your Life and More.*

3/4: Figure out what motivates you the most and then add that to your morning routine... play your favorite music, do something on your To Do list, read an inspirational quote or go for an enjoyable walk.

3/5: Are you having a hard time deciding what you want to keep and what items need to go? Remember... *"Clutter is the physical manifestation of unmade decisions fueled by procrastination." Christina Scalise, OrganizeYourLifeAndMore.com* ... so make some organizing and clutter removing decisions today!

✒ **3/6:** Clean out the kitchen drawers today; take everything out, toss what you no longer want or need, wipe down the inside of each drawer and place the items you want to keep back in an organized manner.

✒ **3/7:** In honor of National Procrastination week. Stop procrastinating and work on that ONE task (or make that one decision) you've been putting off for so long.

✒ **3/8:** Toss anything you no longer need, clean off the top of your desk by removing as much as possible, organize all desk drawers and office supplies (storing the items you use most often within reach) and then toss, file, or shred any papers as necessary.

✒ **3/9:** Go through your email inbox and unsubscribe to those you no longer want to receive. Then, respond to, delete or file as many emails as possible.

✒ **3/10:** Go through your collection of movies, music and books (including all digital files) and discard the ones you no longer enjoy.

✒ **3/11:** Take one or more boxes out of storage, go through them thoroughly today and toss anything you no longer want or need.

✒ **3/12:** Find a few motivational quotes you enjoy and post them around your home and office today.

✒ **3/13:** Wash all garbage cans inside and out today.

✒ **3/14:** Search for a new cell phone app or computer program that will help make life a little easier and then take the time to learn how to use it.

✓ **3/15:** What kinds of clutter do you deal with most; physical, digital, mental? Figure out which types of clutter are affecting your life the most and work on ways to reduce that clutter today. * *For more great organizing tips, check out my newest organizing book... Organize Your Life and More.*

✓ **3/16:** Shampoo the rugs and/or furniture in your home today.

✓ **3/17:** Find one or more items in your home that have been sitting out for awhile and put them away where they belong...for items that don't have a designated storage spot, create one.

✓ **3/18:** Organize all painting supplies. Toss or recycle items you no longer need or use and lable all remaining paint cans with the corresponding rooms in your home. **For more information on how to organize "Paint, Paint Supplies, and Paint Samples" please refer to Chapter 21 of Organize Your Life and More.*

✓ **3/19:** Clean the area underneath your sink today.

✓ **3/20:** Neaten the workspace at home or in your office... label a few items, drawers or files so that everyone (who utilizes that space) will be able to quickly find what they are looking for.

✓ **3/21:** Clean out the garage. Get rid of all unwanted items and then organize the rest.

✓ **3/22:** Search your home and try to find five or more items (clothes, knick-knacks, gadgets, coffee mugs, books, movies, etc.) your family no longer wants or needs; then toss, sell or donate those items.

3/23: Go through the supplies in your laundry room. Get rid of the items you no longer need then organize the remaining items together into categories...detergents, fabric softeners, stain fighters, etc.

3/24: Do one or more things on your personal To Do list today.

3/25: Clean all mirrors in your home today.

3/26: Wash all curtains and windows in your home today.

3/27: Toss all worn out t-shirts, socks and under garments. *Note: Old t-shirts and socks make great cleaning rags ...and old socks can also be used as "sock puppet cleaning rags" to help motivate young children to help with household cleaning – simply draw a face on the sock using a permanent marker and then have your child use their sock puppet to help "destroy the dirt".*

3/28: Gather all cleaning supplies together into one place, decide what can be thrown out and the next time you clean, use up the ones with the least amount left in them first.

3/29: Deep clean all major appliances inside and out today; refrigerator, stove, microwave, dishwasher and more.

3/30: Clean out the pantry; wipe down shelves, toss all expired items and categorize the remaining items into separate areas of your pantry; cereals, canned goods, paper products, snacks, soups, sauces, drinks, condiments, pastas and more.

3/31: Take the day off today, enjoy what you've already organized and spend some time with friends and/or family.

April is...
National Stress Awareness month / Car Care month / Pest Management month
Third week of April is... National Organize Your Files week

✓ **4/1:** It's National Stress Awareness month... What are you stressed out about the most...work, kids, clutter, health, finances? Spend a few minutes today and try to find a few ways to improve those situations; and then find a few ways to reduce the stress connected to each one.

✓ **4/2:** Have you filed your taxes? The tax filing deadline is coming up soon (usually April 15th each year); if you haven't filed your taxes yet, work on getting that done today.

✓ **4/3:** Schedule in some time for *yourself* every day (even if it's only for a few minutes); go for a walk, start exercising, sit down and enjoy a meal instead of rushing through it, listen to your favorite music or simply lay on the ground outside and watch the clouds roll by.

✓ **4/4:** Find a nice bucket or basket to carry all of your gardening supplies and outdoor tools.

✓ **4/5:** Try out a new recipe today and adjust the ingredients if necessary. Then, make notes as to how well your family enjoyed it and file it away under the corresponding category. If no one liked it, simply toss the recipe.

✓ **4/6:** What can you organize today that would make the most positive impact on your life right now...your home, your office, your finances, your schedule? Get working on it today!

✓ **4/7:** Clean out your vehicle; vacuum and wipe down the inside, toss any trash, straighten out all compartments and add any roadside emergency supplies if necessary.

✔ **4/8:** Reduce your daily stress level...create a list of things to smile about (family pictures, favorite quotes or fun reminders) and then post your list where you will see it daily.

✔ **4/9:** Shop around and compare prices on insurance; car, life, home owner's insurance... could you be saving money by switching insurance companies?

✔ **4/10:** Time for a yearly check, for insect and pest problems around your home. Get ahead of any potential problems *before* they get out of control. Find and destroy bees' nests that are starting to form, lay out ant and mouse traps, protect your pets with updated shots and flea and tick control products; and then take time to block off any small holes where insects and pests may be entering your home.

✔ **4/11:** Clean out your refrigerator and freezer today. Toss all expired items, wipe down the entire refrigerator inside and out and defrost the freezer if necessary.

✔ **4/12:** It's time to swap out the outdoor furniture and décor; start unpacking your springtime stuff and then pack away the winter items for the season.

✔ **4/13:** Search your home and try to find five or more items (clothes, knick-knacks, gadgets, coffee mugs, books, movies, etc.) your family no longer wants or needs; then toss, sell or donate those items.

✅ **4/14:** Look over your current household filing system and find one or more ways to improve it in a way that works best for you and your family...place them in alphabetical order, stagger the files so each tab can be seen (and found) easily and/or group them together into categories such as medical and health records, general accounts, monthly bills, investments, insurance, taxes, etc.

✅ **4/15:** Consider adding a pocket folder or binder to your vehicle that will hold and organize those frequently used restaurant menus, store coupons and more.

✅ **4/16:** If you are lacking storage space in your kitchen, find items you've stocked up on or that are used less often and store them in a different area of your home... the closer to the kitchen, the better. For example: a simple shelving unit or storage cabinet placed in another room, a closet or even in the basement area close by can help free up a lot of storage space in your kitchen.

✅ **4/17:** Choose one room in your home and clean the entire room from top to bottom. Clean the baseboards, windows, walls, floors, furniture and light fixtures, get rid of any unwanted items and for each item you find that does not have a storage place; create one.

✅ **4/18:** Check the maintenance record on your vehicle. Is it due for an oil change? Is it time to rotate the tires? Is it ready for the summer? Schedule in some time for any necessary maintenance - today.

✅ **4/19:** Create a file folder for each home project you are currently working on and place all corresponding paperwork inside each one. Example: If you are currently redecorating a room in your home...place all paint color swatches, supply receipts, magazine cut outs and more, into one project folder.

✓ **4/20:** Clean your outdoor grill today.

✓ **4/21:** Start planning a family vacation or a quick getaway. Gather the family together, discuss where you would like to go, check your schedules, pick a day/week to do it, then start shopping around for the best deals.

✓ **4/22:** Do one or more things on your personal To Do list today.

✓ **4/23:** Take the day off today, enjoy what you've already organized and spend some time with friends and/or family.

✓ **4/24:** Clean up the lawn today. Pick up trash, rocks, debris and more.

✓ **4/25:** Find one or more items in your home that have been sitting out for awhile and put them away where they belong...for items that don't have a designated storage spot, create one.

✓ **4/26:** Take some time today to finish a task or project (large or small) that you've been putting off for a while now.

✓ **4/27:** Choose one or more cabinets to clean out today (kitchen, laundry room, bathroom, etc.) Take everything out, wipe down each shelf, get rid of unwanted items, group like items together and then place everything back into the cabinet in an organized manner.

✓ **4/28:** Create a bill paying system that will help remind you when each bill is due...or find ways to improve your current system. ** For more information on Finances, creating a budget and paying bills - please see Chapter 12 of Organize Your Life and More.*

4/29: Avoid television, computers and cell phones as much as possible this week and find fun, productive things to do instead.

4/30: Start planning your outdoor gardening...decide on what you want to grow this year, where you want to plant your garden, purchase the necessary seeds and start preparing the soil.

May is...
Scrapbook month / Revise Your Work Schedule month
First full week of May is... Be Kind to Animals week

✎ **5/1:** Create or update an existing To Do list for yourself and a chores sheet for your children. Then get started on both today.

✎ **5/2:** Check all summertime equipment such as lawn mowers, weed trimmers, chainsaws and barbeques for any needed maintenance and repair; then schedule in some time to get it all done.

✎ **5/3:** Go through your books and magazines and get rid of those you no longer want. Toss, sell or donate what you can to your local library, school or charity and then unsubscribe to the magazines you no longer want or have time to read.

✎ **5/4:** Check your supply of sunscreen, bug spray, bandages and medical supplies; do you need to toss and/or replace any of them?

✎ **5/5:** Are you ready for Mother's Day weekend? If you haven't hit the stores yet, avoid the weekend shopping madness and get it done today.

✎ **5/6:** In honor of Be Kind to Animals week...take time to pamper your pets and donate a few items to your local animal shelter. Most shelters have a list of items they are in need of, posted directly on their websites and include items such as...old blankets, pet food, pet toys, paper towels, laundry detergent and more. To find out what your local shelter is in need of...check their website or simply give them a call today.

✅ **5/7:** Don't have time to run to the bank, but often find yourself needing change for a specific payment or transaction? Consider adding an envelope of cash to your household safe that includes all denominations...$20, $10, $5 & $1 bills and coins.

✅ **5/8:** Go through your closet and get rid of any items that are unwanted, outdated, worn out or no longer fit...pants, shoes, shirts, coats, hats, scarves, gloves and more.

✅ **5/9:** Inspect the outside of your home for any necessary repairs and maintenance, then start a To Do list with the things that will need to be done.

✅ **5/10:** Find ways to simplify your work schedule so you will have more time for family and friends. For example: change your work hours (go in earlier, so you can get out earlier), find a shorter route to and from work or work four days a week doing 10 hour shifts instead of five days a week working 8 hour shifts.

✅ **5/11:** Search your home and try to find five or more items (clothes, knick-knacks, gadgets, coffee mugs, books, movies, etc.) your family no longer wants or needs; then toss, sell or donate those items.

✅ **5/12:** Check your indoor plants today. Are they all still alive and well? Do they need bigger pots, fresh water or dirt? Or, maybe they would look better in a different area of your home...do a little indoor gardening today.

✅ **5/13:** Go through your email inbox and unsubscribe to those you no longer want to receive. Then, respond to, delete or file as many emails as possible.

✓ **5/14:** Take the day off today, enjoy what you've already organized and spend some time with friends and/or family.

✓ **5/15:** Go through your family photos. Toss and delete the ones you no longer want to keep and then organize the remaining ones into photo albums, picture frames and computer files.

✓ **5/16:** Clean all outdoor furniture today.

✓ **5/17:** Dispose or recycle all paint cans, oil containers and cleaners you no longer want or need. *Check with your local municipality or recycling center for more information on how and where to properly dispose of these items.*

✓ **5/18:** Challenge yourself to throw out as many unwanted coffee mugs, glasses and cups as you can today.

✓ **5/19:** Clean out your medicine cabinet and properly dispose of all expired medications. *For proper medication disposal please check the FDA website for more information…* http://www.fda.gov/ForConsumers/ConsumerUpdates/ucm101653.htm

✓ **5/20:** Find one or more items in your home that have been sitting out for awhile and put them away where they belong…for items that don't have a designated storage spot, create one.

✓ **5/21:** Is it time for a new piece of furniture in your home? If so, consider looking for one with storage features. If you currently have furniture with storage compartments already in them, take some time to clean them out today.

✓ **5/22:** Check the gutters on your home and clean out any debris.

5/23: Clean the cobwebs from every area of your home today including your attic, basement and garage.

5/24: Do one or more things on your personal To Do list today.

5/25: Go through all bathroom supplies and toss the ones you no longer use, want or need. Sort and organize the rest.

5/26: Start clearing out all those boxes of unwanted items today...plan a garage sale, sell a few items online or finally take some time to make a trip to your local charity and make that donation.

5/27: Choose any drawer in your home (kitchen, bathroom, dresser, etc.) and toss the items you no longer want or need, then sort and organize the rest.

5/28: Have each family member find one or more items they no longer want or need and toss, sell or donate those items immediately.

5/29: Freshen the look of one or more rooms in your home today... rearrange the furniture, update the décor, repaint the walls and have fun with it.

5/30: Find one area of your home that is lacking storage space (for example: in the bathroom, kitchen or bedroom, under the stairs or in a closet) and purge a few items you no longer want or need in that area, install shelving, hang a few things up or simply go vertical with your storage ideas.

5/31: Organize your scrapbooking, craft and/or sewing supplies today; make sure to toss what you no longer want or need in the process.

June is...
Effective Communications Month

✔ **6/1:** It's Effective Communications Month. Set up a communication area at work; hang a poster board for general information and provide small cubbies with each person's name to leave each other notes, paperwork, incoming mail and more.

✔ **6/2:** Label a few items in your home (file folders, storage containers, freezer items and more) making sure all labels are clearly written or printed, facing forward, easily visible and thoroughly describing the contents inside.

✔ **6/3:** Repair, replace or toss one broken item in your home today.

✔ **6/4:** Find a new cell phone app you may want to try, that helps you share crucial information such as calendars and shopping lists with family, friends and/or coworkers.

✔ **6/5:** Set up a family communication area somewhere in your home. Hang a dry erase and/or magnetic board for posting information, notes and schedules. Then, set up shelving or cubbies where you can leave each other items such as clothing, incoming mail and returned items.

✔ **6/6:** Dust and/or wipe down the walls inside your home.

✔ **6/7:** Find a stack of papers that have been sitting around for a while and take care of each piece of paper in that pile immediately...recycle, toss, shred, file or finish any necessary tasks related to the papers involved.

✍ **6/8:** Avoid last minute shopping for Father's Day. If you plan on making a gift or doing something special; get it done today.

✍ **6/9:** Choose one room in your home and clean the entire room from top to bottom. Clean the baseboards, windows, walls, floors, furniture and light fixtures, get rid of any unwanted items and for each item you find that does not have a storage place; create one.

✍ **6/10:** Update your calendar today. Have you forgotten to add anything? Do you need a different calendar system that works better for you and your family. *Note: If you have never used Google calendars before, take the time to check them out today.*

✍ **6/11:** Hold a family meeting to discuss what areas of your lives need organizing the most...schedules, finances, bedrooms, kitchen, etc... then work on improving them together.

✍ **6/12:** Change the air / furnace filters in your home. *Experts recommend <u>checking</u> your filters once a month; and <u>changing</u> them whenever they are dirty (or a minimum of every three months).*

✍ **6/13:** Constantly dealing with tough stains in your laundry pile? Create a stain remedy list and post it next to your washing machine for quick and easy reference.

✍ **6/14:** Do one or more things on your personal To Do list today.

✍ **6/15:** Avoid wasting time talking to telemarketers; register your phone number(s) with the National Do Not Call Registry online.... https://www.donotcall.gov/

✓ **6/16:** Vacuum and/or wipe down all lights and lamp shades today.

✓ **6/17:** Search your home and try to find five or more items (clothes, knick-knacks, gadgets, coffee mugs, books, movies, etc.) your family no longer wants or needs; then toss, sell or donate those items.

✓ **6/18:** Take the day off today, enjoy what you've already organized and spend some time with friends and/or family.

✓ **6/19:** Organize your extra sets of bed sheets today. Place the entire set into one pillow case for easy storage and sort by size (twin, full, queen and king).

✓ **6/20:** Sort through your office supplies today. Toss what you no longer want or need; and then organize the rest.

✓ **6/21:** Find one or more items in your home that have been sitting out for awhile and put them away where they belong...for items that don't have a designated storage spot, create one.

✓ **6/22:** Go through all of your "Miscellaneous" hardware; toss what you no longer need and sort and organize the rest. *Note: For tips on how to organize all those small hardware items...please see Chapter 21, of Organize Your Life and More..."Ten Ways to Organize those Smallest of Items".*

✓ **6/23:** Take time today to finally make that phone call; or return that email you've been putting off for so long.

✓ **6/24:** Go through all of your reminder/post-it notes, follow up on a few of them and then toss the ones you no longer need.

✓ **6/25:** Sort through your jewelry box today and decide what you no longer want to keep; then organize the rest.

✓ **6/26:** Clean your basement and/or attic today. Toss, donate or sell those items you no longer want or need.

✓ **6/27:** For those clothes you've only worn once but aren't quite ready to wash yet... designate one shelf in your closet for them ...or hang them on different colored hangers ...or hang them on hangers that face in the opposite direction.

✓ **6/28:** Get help with a large project (or several small tasks) by hiring a professional, enlisting the help of family or friends or by simply posting a Help Wanted sign for the kids. *Note: for an example "Help Wanted" sign for your kids, please see Chapter 4 of Organize Your Life and More... "Help Wanted".*

✓ **6/29:** Encourage your child's independence; designate one or more easy to reach drawers and/or shelves for storing their items... in the kitchen, bathroom, laundry room and more.

✓ **6/30:** Gather all take-out menus, place them into a labeled binder or folder and then, store them in an area that makes sense to you and your family.

July is...
Purposeful Parenting month

7/1: Cure boredom by creating a written list of Fun Things To Do; then encourage your kids to change and add to it often. *For an example list of "Fun Things to Do" for kids, please see Chapter 15 of Organize Your Life and More.*

7/2: Work on one small home repair project today.

7/3: Do last minute shopping for any upcoming Independence Day celebrations.

7/4: Take the day off today, enjoy what you've already organized and spend some time with friends and/or family.

7/5: Encourage organization and independence by providing your children with file folders and a file cabinet, box or drawer of their own. Once they've decided which papers they'd like to file away, help them decide how to label each file folder and then show them how to sort their papers inside each one. Example: oldest papers always go in the back of the file and newest ones always go in the front. *Note: Storing a few empty folders in the back (or front) of a file cabinet gives your child quick and easy access to new and empty files they may need in the future...and helps encourage the continued use of their new filing system.*

7/6: Encourage your children to start thinking about their future. Ask them about careers they may be interested in, help them research information on each one (job details, salaries, colleges they may want to attend and more) and then have them get an insider's view of each career choice by talking with a few people who are currently working in those professions.

✓ **7/7:** Take one or more boxes out of storage, go through them thoroughly today and toss anything you no longer want or need.

✓ **7/8:** Go through your collection of body lotions, sprays and colognes; toss the ones you no longer use.

✓ **7/9:** What area of your home could benefit the most from becoming organized? Work on that area today.

✓ **7/10:** Review your family budget; then help your child create a budget of their own so *they* can start planning ahead for their own future. *See Chapter 12 of Organize Your Life and More for an example family budget and Chapter 15 for example budgets for teenagers and young children.*

✓ **7/11:** Go through your email inbox and unsubscribe to those you no longer want to receive. Then, respond to, delete or file as many emails as possible.

✓ **7/12:** Discuss schedules and assignments of household chores with all family members today. If necessary, make modifications to help accommodate preferences and changing schedules.

✓ **7/13:** Find one area of your family budget where you can cut back and save money; then have your kids do the same with their own personal budgets.

✓ **7/14:** Post helpful household tips where your family needs them the most. Example: post instructions on how to use the washing machine for younger family members who are still learning how to do their own laundry.

✍ **7/15:** Search your home and try to find five or more items (clothes, knick-knacks, gadgets, coffee mugs, books, movies, etc.) your family no longer wants or needs; then toss, sell or donate those items.

✍ **7/16:** Find an area in your home where you are wasting space; then find a way to utilize that space...some areas to consider checking...under the stairs, behind doors, inside cabinets and under shelves.

✍ **7/17:** Create a binder of your "Favorite Family Recipes" and have your child create one of their own as well. Then, help them find recipes they may enjoy adding to it and encourage them to make one or more of those recipes each week. *For specific instructions on how to create a recipe binder please see Chapter 19 of Organize Your Life and More.*

✍ **7/18:** Choose one or more cabinets to clean out today (kitchen, laundry room, bathroom, etc.) Take everything out, wipe down each shelf, get rid of unwanted items, group like items together and then place everything back into the cabinet in an organized manner.

✍ **7/19:** What do you collect; stuffed animals, baseball cards, books? Reevaluate your collections and see how many items you can part with today.

✍ **7/20:** Find one or more items in your home that have been sitting out for awhile and put them away where they belong...for items that don't have a designated storage spot, create one.

✍ **7/21:** Vacuum behind and underneath your furniture today.

7/22: Sort through your washcloths, sheets, blankets, hand and bath towels; toss those you no longer want or need. *If you want to donate your unwanted linens to a good cause - consider checking with your local animal shelter to see if they can use them.*

7/23: Clean / wipe-down all doors and doorways inside your home today.

7/24: Give yourself a break, and your children an opportunity to earn some extra cash and/or privileges...create a list of Extra Jobs that need to be done around your home, what you're willing to give in return for doing each task (cash, extra privileges or special rewards), post it in a high traffic area, update it frequently (for example: every morning or once a week) and encourage your kids to check it out often. *For an example list of "Extra Jobs" for kids, please see Chapter 15 of Organize Your Life and More.*

7/25: Help your child pick up and organize their room. As an extra incentive, ask them to think about ways they'd like to redecorate it when they're done.

7/26: What can you organize today that would make the most positive impact on your life right now...your office, your finances, your schedule? Get working on it today!

7/27: Combat the weeds in your garden, lawn or driveway today.

7/28: Do one or more things on your personal To Do list today.

7/29: Combat boredom...fill a "Busy Bag" with reading material, games and toys for those times when you and the kids are stuck waiting around in places like doctor's offices and grocery store lines with nothing fun to do.

7/30: Dust all picture frames, knick-knacks, hanging lights and baseboards.

7/31: Does your child have a special talent? Artwork, jewelry, music, sewing, crafts??? Help them find ways to turn their creativity into cash, an enjoyable hobby ...or both.

August is...
Happiness Happens month
First week of August is... Simplify Your Life week

8/1: Discuss meal planning ideas with your family during dinner tonight and try to find recipes that include items you already have on hand and need to use up before they expire.

8/2: Cook in bulk today. Prepare twice the amount of dinner you will need for tonight and then freeze half of it for a quick and easy meal another night. Be sure it's something that will freeze well such as meatloaf, potpies, enchiladas, burritos, lasagna, casseroles, pasta sauce, meatballs, breaded chicken or pork, soups and stews.

8/3: Are you frequently overwhelmed by everything you need to do? If so, reevaluate your schedule and find one or more things you can either eliminate or change that will make life just a little bit easier...starting today!

8/4: Give yourself one more reasons to smile each day...create a collage of things that make you feel happy and inspired...inspirational quotes, funny pictures, words of wisdom and more...then post it where it will be seen each morning.

8/5: For those of you who have Queen and King size fitted sheets and can never remember which corner goes where...try using permanent marker on the corner tag of the sheet and write down which end of the bed that particular corner should be placed on. For example: mark the tag with "LB" for left bottom corner of the bed or "LB/RT" if it can go in either the left bottom or right top corners of the bed. *Note: If there's no tag available to write on and you don't mind having small letters written directly on the sheets, you can do that as well.*

8/6: To save time when replacing garbage bags, place a few extra bags at the bottom of each garbage can.

8/7: Do you keep purchasing the same item over and over again because you always have trouble finding it when you need it the most? For example... you need a screwdriver for a small repair job, search your entire home and can't find it. So, you go to the store, purchase a new one, get the job done and then (a few days later) find the screwdriver you were originally looking for in the one spot you didn't think to look. If this happens to you often, take time today to organize that one specific area of your home so finding that one item will no longer be a challenge. Be sure to categorize all like items together in a place that will make sense to both you and your family, and make sure each item is clearly visible. And, if you discover you have more than you need (or want to keep), donate or sell a few of those extra items immediately.

8/8: Search your home and try to find five or more items (clothes, knick-knacks, gadgets, coffee mugs, books, movies, etc.) your family no longer wants or needs; then toss, sell or donate those items.

8/9: Create a list of meal ideas (similar to a restaurant menu) for your family to choose from each week. Then, start making plans for upcoming meals. Decide which meals you'd like to have, who will be making them, add any necessary ingredients to your shopping list and then plan accordingly. And, to keep mealtime from getting boring, every so often, be sure to add new menu options to that list.

8/10: Find a decorative container, bowl or basket to store everyday items such as cell phone, keys and wallet; then place it in an area that works best for you and your family.

8/11: Walk through your home today and look around; can you find a few things that trigger unhappy thoughts, memories or feelings? If you no longer need those items, make your home a happier place by getting rid of them as soon as possible. Then, be sure to display a few items that always create a smile.

8/12: Create a Grab and Go Tool Kit (or update an existing one) for everyday household repairs by placing your most commonly used tools into a small, easy to carry bag or container. Just a few things you may want to include...a hammer, screwdriver (both flat head and phillips head), tape measure and pliers.

8/13: Could you save money and time by bundling your internet, phone and television service? Shop around and compare prices today.

8/14: Find one or more ways to improve, change or advance in your career in a way that makes *you* happy. A few examples: change your work hours, find a way to simplify a few tasks, reorganize your work space or work a little harder towards that next promotion.

8/15: Make it quicker and easier for your family to make healthier food choices by separating the good from the bad in your cupboards and pantry. For example: Organic items on the left side and non-healthy items on the right side. Then search for more healthy and organic alternatives the next time you shop and watch that side of the cupboard or pantry grow.

8/16: Take the day off today, enjoy what you've already organized and spend some time with friends and/or family.

8/17: Find out which supplies your child will need for school this year and add those items to your shopping list.

✓ **8/18:** Help your child sort through their entire wardrobe today...clothes, shoes, coats, hats, gloves, scarves and more; get rid of items that no longer fit...or they no longer want or need. Then, create a shopping list of any clothing items they will need for the upcoming school year.

✓ **8/19:** Go through <u>your</u> entire wardrobe today...clothes, shoes, coats, hats, gloves, scarves and more; get rid of items that no longer fit and you no longer want or need.

✓ **8/20:** Clean out the drawers in your bathroom today; take everything out, toss what you no longer want or need, wipe down the inside of each drawer and place the items you want to keep back in an organized manner.

✓ **8/21:** Choose one room in your home and clean the entire room from top to bottom. Clean the baseboards, windows, walls, floors, furniture and light fixtures, get rid of any unwanted items and for each item you find that does not have a storage place; create one.

✓ **8/22:** What are your dreams? Where would you like to travel? What would you like to accomplish? Create (or update) a Life Goals List, Bucket List or collage and start finding ways to make your dreams a reality today!

✓ **8/23:** Find one or more items in your home that have been sitting out for awhile and put them away where they belong...for items that don't have a designated storage spot, create one.

✔ **8/24:** Untangle, neaten and then label (if necessary) all hanging wires and cords in your home. There are so many ways you can do this using stickers, tags, clips and silver/black markers. Check Pinterest and/or Google for today's newest ideas.

✔ **8/25:** Do one or more things on your personal To Do list today.

✔ **8/26:** Find those items that are constantly being tossed on the floor and create a permanent drop spot for them for when they're not being used. For example: If your child is constantly throwing their school stuff (backpacks, bags, books, coat, etc.) on the floor in their bedroom, create a catch all drop spot for them using one or more of the following...a coat rack, cubbies, small end table, desk or a few hooks installed on the side of a shelving unit or on the wall.

✔ **8/27:** Have each family member find one or more items they no longer want or need and toss, sell or donate those items immediately.

✔ **8/28:** Supply items such as food, paper products, cleaners, first-aid supplies, office supplies and more can *all* pile up very quickly. Take time today to figure out what you DO and DO NOT have in stock; and adjust your next shopping list accordingly. And, if you find you had to dig through the items to figure it all out... it may be time to reorganize your supplies. All supply items should be placed into categories with all like items stored together in the same area. After you've reorganized...if you find you have too many of one particular item, slowly work on using up what you already have in stock or donate the ones you don't think you will be able to use.

✔ **8/29:** Review and update any existing chores and rules sheets you may have for your kids, so their responsibilities at home don't conflict and interfere with their school schedules, after-school activities and homework time.

✔ **8/30:** Find ways to use television time wisely...check emails, fold laundry, sew or knit, exercise, create a Shopping or To Do list, clip coupons, sort through old boxes of stuff, clean out a drawer....you'd be surprised at what you can accomplish during the time it takes to watch one television show!

✔ **8/31:** Clean out and organize your laundry room area...toss all products you no longer use, store similar items together and set up separate laundry baskets for darks, whites and rinse loads.

September is...
Back to School Time
National Preparedness month
September 6th is...Fight Procrastination Day

✓ **9/1:** Update your list of emergency contact information (phone numbers, addresses, etc.) in all family members' cell phones and make sure <u>all</u> emergency numbers have also been posted in one central location of your home.

✓ **9/2:** Have your kids create their own morning checklists to remind them of everything they need to do and bring with them each day.

✓ **9/3:** Wash all curtains and windows in your home today.

✓ **9/4:** Take some time and finally finish that project you started a long time ago.

✓ **9/5:** Hang a few things up today to create more storage space. And, if you haven't discovered Command Strips yet, check them out...they are simply wonderful!

✓ **9/6:** Today is Fight Procrastination Day... walk around your home and start making decisions about each item of clutter TODAY! Examples: Where should the item be stored? What is the most efficient way to store this item? Should I keep it, toss it or donate it? Remember... *"Clutter is the physical manifestation of unmade decisions fueled by procrastination" Christina Scalise, Organize Your Life and More.*

✓ **9/7:** For busier days when your family is rushing out the door...set up a Healthy Grab and Go Snack basket in both your pantry and refrigerator. * *For a list of Grab and Go Snack ideas, please see Chapter 19 of Organize Your Life and More.*

✍ **9/8:** Review your current car insurance policy. Is it up to date? Do you need to make any changes? Are you paying too much? If so, find out if you qualify for any discounts. If not, start shopping around for a better rate.

✍ **9/9:** Review your current home owner's (or rental) insurance policy and make updates if necessary. Do you have enough coverage? Do you qualify for any discounts that may not be included in your current policy? Can you get a better rate through a different company? Find out today.

✍ **9/10:** Shampoo the rugs and/or furniture in your home today.

✍ **9/11:** Make sure your final affairs are in order....check your life insurance policies, will and more to ensure they are all up-to-date. *Please see Chapter 11 of Organize Your Life and More for more information on how to get your "Final Affairs in Order" and what to do upon the "Death of a Loved One".*

✍ **9/12:** Do you find yourself consistently looking for the same lost item over and over again? For frequently misplaced items...take the time to find, and then designate a permanent storage spot for those items. Then, place them where they belong whenever they are not being used.

✍ **9/13:** Update the emergency kit(s) in your vehicle(s). Just a few of the items you may want to include...blanket, water, dry snacks that can withstand extreme temperatures, cell phone charger, bungee cords, rope, tow strap, windshield washer fluid, first-aid kit, road-side flares, jumper cables, jack, flashlight (wind-up or one with fresh batteries), small fire extinguisher, tire gauge and spare tire.

✓ **9/14:** Search your home and try to find five or more items (clothes, knick-knacks, gadgets, coffee mugs, books, movies, etc.) your family no longer wants or needs; then toss, sell or donate those items.

✓ **9/15:** Sort through all of the extra cords, wires and chargers that haven't been used in awhile...such as...old extension cords, left-over pieces from a wiring job, chargers for cell phones, ipods, game systems, televisions and satellite cables....how many of these items can you get rid of?

✓ **9/16:** Sort through all backpacks, purses, hand bags and luggage; toss those you no longer want to keep.

✓ **9/17:** Go through your email inbox and unsubscribe to those you no longer want to receive. Then, respond to, delete or file as many emails as possible.

✓ **9/18:** Clean the outside of your home today...siding, windows, light fixtures, porch/deck, gutters, chimney, etc.

✓ **9/19:** Take time today to clean out your spice cabinet or drawer. Toss the ones that have expired and then reorganize the remaining spices, in a way that works best for the people who use them the most.

✓ **9/20:** Create (or update) your family's communication board/area to make sure information is flowing in the most effective and efficient way possible.

✓ **9/21:** Do one or more things on your personal To Do list today.

✓ **9/22:** Create a drop spot area for items that are brought in and out of your home on a daily basis; such as keys, cell phones, gym bags, lunch pails, backpacks, etc.

✍ **9/23:** Go through your closet and get rid of any items that are unwanted, outdated, worn out or no longer fit...pants, shoes, shirts, coats, hats, scarves, gloves and more.

✍ **9/24:** Take the day off today, enjoy what you've already organized and spend some time with friends and/or family.

✍ **9/25:** Are you prepared if you suddenly lose power in your home? Do you have enough candles, lighters and matches on hand? Do your flashlights need new batteries? Do you have extra batteries on hand? Are your emergency kits stored in a place that is easily accessible; will you be able to find them in the dark? For more information on how to prepare for a blackout, please visit... https://www.ready.gov/power-outages.

✍ **9/26:** Find one or more items in your home that have been sitting out for awhile and put them away where they belong...for items that don't have a designated storage spot, create one.

✍ **9/27:** Look over your Shopping lists and To Do lists. What errands and/or small jobs can you consolidate and get done today?

✍ **9/28:** Review your current investments and/or retirement plans. Can you find ways to improve them?

✍ **9/29:** Make that trip to your local charity and donate your unwanted items today. If you can't possibly do it today, schedule in a time when you can.

9/30: Collect all magazines and newspapers; recycle as many as possible. For ones you still want to read, or simply skim through...find time to go through them before bed, while watching television, or bring them with you to places where you'll be waiting around with nothing else to do.

October is...
National Organize Your Medical Information Month
National Fire Prevention Month
The Week (Sunday through Saturday) in which October 9th falls is... National Fire Prevention Week

☑ **10/1:** Time to donate more unwanted items... Most animal shelters are in need old blankets, rugs, pet toys, pet food, dishes, cages and more. Find out what your local animal shelter is in need of (call or look them up online) and then find some items to donate today.

☑ **10/2:** Organize your family's medical information for quick and easy reference. Set up folders (or three ring binders) for each family member with the following information...name, birth date, blood type, allergies, current medications, pharmacy, physician names & contact information, preferred hospital, dental and optical records and information, health insurance information, health history (illnesses, injuries, immunizations, procedures/surgeries, chronic conditions, lab/test dates and results, past medications, doctor's visits, family history and lifestyle habits), copies of Health Care Proxy, Living Will, Power of Attorney, organ donation authorization and list of emergency contacts.

☑ **10/3:** Create or update an existing Home Maintenance schedule for items that need regular maintenance; furnace, chimney, air conditioner, water tanks, septic system and more. Then add reminders to your calendar for each one.

☑ **10/4:** Go through your Halloween and Thanksgiving decorations today and toss, recycle or donate those you no longer enjoy.

☑ **10/5:** Sort through your coat closets and donate or sell what you no longer use or need.

10/6: Take time today to find a solution to a current household problem you've been dealing with. <u>Example:</u> Your family can never remember how to properly use that one piece of equipment that is used so infrequently. Solution: Type up a simple set of instructions and post it near the item itself or adhere an instruction label directly onto the item.

10/7: Find a stack of papers that have been sitting around for a while and take care of each piece of paper in that pile immediately...recycle, toss, shred, file or finish any necessary tasks related to the papers involved.

10/8: Organize your keys today. Toss the ones you no longer need and then label the ones you plan to keep. Use different styles of keys or different colored key covers for quick identification.

10/9: Are you prepared for a fire? Plan at least two different escape routes for each family member...practice it regularly, make sure any obstacles have been removed and designate a place for your family to meet. Other things you can do... practice Stop, Drop and Roll and crawling or crouching low to the floor in a smoke filled room.

10/10: Check all smoke and carbon monoxide detectors to ensure they are working properly. Batteries should be replaced a minimum of once per year.

10/11: Change the air / furnace filters in your home. *Experts recommend <u>checking</u> your filters once a month; and <u>changing</u> them whenever they are dirty (or a minimum of every three months).*

✅ **10/12:** Search your home and try to find five or more items (clothes, knick-knacks, gadgets, coffee mugs, books, movies, etc.) your family no longer wants or needs; then toss, sell or donate those items.

✅ **10/13:** Clean, dust and/or vacuum all of the air vents in your home.

✅ **10/14:** Clean out the inside of your clothes dryer vent and lint trap thoroughly today.

✅ **10/15:** Time to evaluate all you've organized so far. Are your new organizational systems working out well for you and your family? Do you need to adjust any of them to make things work out a little better? If so, work on that today.

✅ **10/16:** Time to get ready for winter and pack away the last of those summer items. What can you do to prepare? Stock up on supplies, winterize your home and outdoor equipment, clean your chimney and more. The more you do ahead of time, the less stressful the winter months will be.

✅ **10/17:** Wash all cabinet _doors_ inside and out...kitchen, bathroom, laundry room, etc. Don't forget to wash the handles too!

✅ **10/18:** Look inside each bathroom and kitchen cabinet. Where are you losing space? Find ways to maximize your storage space by reorganizing your cabinets today. * *For more information on "Creative Storage", "Wasted Spaces" or how to find "Hidden Storage Hiding in Your Cabinets" please see Chapter 7 of Organize Your Life and More.*

10/19: Store more items where you can SEE them. Keep things visible on shelves (smaller items in front of larger items) and consider using clearly marked labels and clear storage containers (for food, clothing, keepsakes and more). Remember, if you can SEE it, you will FIND it much quicker and easier.

10/20: Find one or more items in your home that have been sitting out for awhile and put them away where they belong...for items that don't have a designated storage spot, create one.

10/21: Do one or more things on your personal To Do list today.

10/22: There are many ways to safely organize usernames and passwords these days. Find a way that works best for you that is both secure and convenient.

10/23: Choose one room in your home and clean the entire room from top to bottom. Clean the baseboards, windows, walls, floors, furniture and light fixtures, get rid of any unwanted items and for each item you find that does not have a storage place; create one.

10/24: Find a new way to save money on upcoming purchases...check sale flyers, start using coupons, search for deals online, download a new app for your cell phone or simply learn the art of negotiation.

10/25: Time to flip and/or rotate the mattresses on your beds. Check your manufacturer's guidelines for proper instructions.

✓ **10/26:** Label a few storage boxes in your garage, attic and/or cellar so you will be able to quickly find what you need, when you need it.

✓ **10/27:** Choose one or more cabinets to clean out today (kitchen, laundry room, bathroom, etc.) Take everything out, wipe down each shelf, get rid of unwanted items, group like items together and then place everything back into the cabinet in an organized manner.

✓ **10/28:** Check your family's health records. Is it time for an annual physical, dental cleaning or eye exam? If so, make those appointments today.

✓ **10/29:** Remove as much dust as you can from your home today; don't forget those hanging lights and fans, wall clocks, knick-knacks, picture frames and baseboards.

✓ **10/30:** Inspect the inside of your home for any needed repairs and start a To Do list, if necessary.

✓ **10/31:** Take the day off today, enjoy what you've already organized and spend some time with friends and/or family.

November is...
National Clean Out Your Refrigerator month
November 15th is... National America Recycles day

11/1: Clean out your purse or wallet today.

11/2: When decorating for the upcoming holidays this year (Thanksgiving, Christmas and New Year's) set aside decorations you no longer want to keep and then donate them to a local charity in need.

11/3: Prepare your shopping list for the upcoming holidays and be sure to start as soon as possible.

11/4: Go through your entire collection of recipes and recipe books, toss those you no longer want to keep and then reorganize the rest.

11/5: Clean out your kitchen utensil drawer today. Remove all items, wipe out the drawer, toss those items you no longer want/need and then place the remaining items back in an organized manner.

11/6: Clean your indoor furniture today.

11/7: Clean out your refrigerator and freezer today. Toss all expired items, wipe down the entire refrigerator inside and out and defrost the freezer if necessary.

11/8: Go through your pantry and kitchen cabinets; toss all expired food items.

11/9: Go through your email inbox and unsubscribe to those you no longer want to receive. Then, respond to, delete or file as many emails as possible.

✓ **11/10:** Schedule a day to get together with friends and exchange items you no longer want or need. This can include books, clothes, movies, music CDs, kitchen gadgets, coffee mugs, candles and much more. To make it fair, have everyone place their items on a table and then take turns choosing one item at a time. At the end of the evening discuss which charities may benefit from the left-over items no one had wanted.

✓ **11/11:** Take the day off today, enjoy what you've already organized and spend some time with friends and/or family.

✓ **11/12:** Break down and recycle all those empty cardboard boxes today.

✓ **11/13:** Discuss this year's holiday gift giving ideas with friends, family and coworkers. Maybe this year, instead of exchanging gifts, you may decide to do something a bit different like....getting together for lunch or a pot luck dinner, collecting items to give to a local charity or exchanging cookies, desserts, plants, flowers or Christmas ornaments (homemade, used or new).

✓ **11/14:** Organize your pantry; place all like items together, pull all older items forward and place the newer ones towards the back. By doing this, you will automatically grab and use the oldest ones first and easily see how much you have left of each item. Once you are done, update your shopping list accordingly.

✓ **11/15:** Today is National America Recycles Day. What can you recycle today?

✍ **11/16:** Go through all of your child's school work and projects that you've held onto throughout the year(s) and toss what you no longer want to keep. For larger projects you simply love but don't want to save, consider taking a picture with your child holding it instead.

✍ **11/17:** Baskets are great for organizing small items. Find a way to reuse an old basket today. Baskets can hold pet toys, newspapers, magazines and much more! *For more ideas on how to Recycle and Reuse...please see Chapter 22 of Organize Your Life and More.*

✍ **11/18:** Get creative today; find an empty container, worn out piece of furniture or some other item that has been lying around your home for a while and figure out how to freshen it up and reuse it in a different way. Check out Pinterest and Google images for some creative ideas to help get you started. One example: An old dresser can be converted into a gift wrapping station by using the drawers to store wrapping paper, gift bags and bows; and the top of the dresser as a place to wrap your gifts.

✍ **11/19:** Clean/dust in those hard to reach places... on top of, behind and underneath the furniture, refrigerator, freezer, washer and dryer, etc.

✍ **11/20:** Prepare next year's calendar by adding in all upcoming appointments, events, birthdays, anniversaries and reminders.

✍ **11/21:** Try out a new recipe today and adjust the ingredients if necessary. Then, make notes as to how well your family enjoyed it and file it away under the corresponding category. If no one liked it, simply toss the recipe.

✅ **11/22:** Do one or more things on your personal To Do list today.

✅ **11/23:** Find one or more items in your home that have been sitting out for awhile and put them away where they belong...for items that don't have a designated storage spot, create one.

✅ **11/24:** Sort through your entire collection of food storage containers and toss or recycle containers and lids that no longer have matches...*or*...use them to organize a loose collection of small items such as makeup, jewelry, office supplies, craft supplies, junk drawer and work bench items.

✅ **11/25:** Clean out underneath the beds and find ways to utilize those areas for storage. Check out under-the-bed storage ideas both in stores and online. And, consider using bed risers or built in storage to add more storage space.

✅ **11/26:** Recycle some old clothes hangers today. You know, the ones you never use but hung onto "just in case" you needed a few more. They may have come from the store, the dry cleaners or were handed down from a friend or family member. Get rid of those you no longer use today.

✅ **11/27:** Have your children find a few toys, video games, stuffed animals and/or movies they no longer want or need; and donate them to a charity in need.

✅ **11/28:** Search your home and try to find five or more items (clothes, knick-knacks, gadgets, coffee mugs, books, movies, etc.) your family no longer wants or needs; then toss, sell or donate those items.

✅ **11/29:** Review last minute preparations for Thanksgiving.

11/30: Practice the one in, one out rule...for every new item brought into your home, toss one or more older items.

December is...
National Stress-Free Family Holiday month
December 31st is... National Make up Your Mind day

✓ **12/1:** To help yourself stay healthy and reduce stress this holiday season, create or update an existing diet and exercise routine...and stick with it.

✓ **12/2:** Sort through your collection of flower vases, candles and décor items; and get rid of the items you no longer want or need.

✓ **12/3:** Have each family member find one or more items they no longer want or need and toss, sell or donate those items immediately.

✓ **12/4:** Go through your collection of old photos; sort and organize those you want to keep and consider making digital copies of your absolute favorites. Would any of them make a good holiday gift for someone special this year?

✓ **12/5:** Check your home for any possible security issues; make sure alarm systems are working, windows and doors are locking properly and everyone in your home has a spare key.

✓ **12/6:** Sort through and organize your gift bags and wrapping paper today; toss items you no longer want or need.

✓ **12/7:** Cut down on morning stress by doing a few things the night before. Prepare lunches, iron clothes, discuss plans and schedules, prepare a morning checklist and leave out items you need to remember to bring with you the next day.

12/8: Choose one room in your home and clean the entire room from top to bottom. Clean the baseboards, windows, walls, floors, furniture and light fixtures, get rid of any unwanted items and for each item you find that does not have a storage place; create one.

12/9: Recharge yourself by taking a few minutes of personal relaxation time today.

12/10: Vacuum behind and underneath your furniture today.

12/11: Time to check your holiday "Shopping" and "To Do" lists. Do you have everything you need? Do you need to make another trip to the store? What else can be done?

12/12: Keep clutter from forming; adjust your schedule to include 5-10 minutes of pick-up time each morning or afternoon and put away as many items as possible within that time period.

12/13: Search your home and try to find five or more items (clothes, knick-knacks, gadgets, coffee mugs, books, movies, etc.) your family no longer wants or needs; then toss, sell or donate those items.

12/14: Find new ways to utilize the time you spend watching television...sew/knit, check emails, fold laundry, update your shopping and To Do lists, go through a box of old stuff, exercise, clip coupons...the list goes on and on.

12/15: Create or update your exercise routine to help make it more enjoyable and rewarding.

✓ **12/16:** Find a new way to relax for a few minutes each day; then include it in your daily schedule...take a walk, read a book, relax by the fire, enjoy a nice hot cup of tea, meditate, listen to your favorite music or spend time enjoying your favorite hobby.

✓ **12/17:** Find a few items in your home that take up valuable shelf space and find a better place to store them. For example: If you've stocked up on canned goods and need more room in your pantry, place a few of them in a separate storage area close by.

✓ **12/18:** Review last minute holiday preparations; check your "Shopping" and "To Do" lists one last time.

✓ **12/19:** Pick up, clean and reorganize your bedroom today. Eliminate what you no longer want or need and make use of any hidden storage spaces.

✓ **12/20:** Sort through your personal grooming and beauty supplies today...cosmetics, shaving supplies, dental care items, nail and hair accessories and more. Toss those you no longer want or use; and organize the rest.

✓ **12/21:** Find one or more items in your home that have been sitting out for awhile and put them away where they belong...for items that don't have a designated storage spot, create one.

✓ **12/22:** Toss kitchen gadgets that are no longer used. Sort and organize the rest.

✓ **12/23:** Find an area in your home where you are wasting space; then find a way to utilize that space...some areas to consider checking...under the stairs, behind doors, inside cabinets and under shelves.

12/24: Do one or more things on your personal To Do list today.

12/25: Take the day off today, enjoy what you've already organized and spend some time with friends and/or family.

12/26: Deep clean all major appliances inside and out today; refrigerator, stove, microwave, dishwasher and more.

12/27: Remove pictures from all cell phones and digital cameras today; save them on your computer and/or external hard drive. And then, back them up using an online service such as Mozy or Carbonite.

12/28: Backup your computer files and make sure they have been protected with the most up to date security software. * *For information on how to protect your computer and personal information, online, please visit...* https://www.irs.gov/uac/seven-tips-to-protect-your-computer-online.

12/29: What can you organize today that would make the most positive impact on your life right now...your office, your finances, your schedule? Get working on it today!

12/30: Do you have items that need to be returned or exchanged at the store? If so, get that done today.

12/31: December 31st is National Make Up Your Mind Day; set aside time for making decisions and setting new goals for the upcoming year.

Congratulations! You did it!
An entire year of organizing, DONE!
So? How do you feel?
More organized? Less stressed? Relieved?
Doesn't it feel great to be organized?!

If you enjoyed this book, please help us spread the word...

Leave a review on the website where you purchased it,
tell a friend or throw us an email at...
organizeyourlifeandmore@gmail.com

Thank you!

About the Author

Christina Scalise is an author, retired Professional Organizer, Reiki Master & Teacher, wife and mother of three.

Want more information?

Websites:
www.OrganizeYourLifeAndMore.com
www.AuthorChristinaScalise.com
www.LightSourceWithin.com

Social networks & other websites:
Facebook, LinkedIn, Twitter, Pinterest, Goodreads & Amazon.

Other Books by Christina Scalise:
Organize Your Life and More
Organize Your Finances, Your Kids, Your Life!
Are We Normal? Funny, True Stories from an Everyday Family
And, contributing author to... 365 Days of Angel Prayers

Made in the USA
Columbia, SC
01 December 2018